Bristol Cranes

A celebration of the cranes in Bristol Harbour

Thomas Rasche

This edition published in 2010 by Redcliffe Press Ltd.,
81g Pembroke Road, Bristol BS8 3EA
www.redcliffepress.co.uk

© Thomas Rasche
www.BristolCranes.co.uk

ISBN 978-1-906593-54-4

A CIP catalogue record for this book is available from the British Library.

Acknowledgements
Andy King, Curator of Industrial and Maritime History for Bristol's Museums, Galleries and Archives, for archive photographs, information and comment.

Illustration credits
p.5   Extract from the 1673 James Millerd map of Bristol: Bristol's Museums, Galleries and Archives.
p.17   Painting by Philip van Dijk: Bristol's Museums, Galleries and Archives.
p.19   Photograph of tower crane on Hannover Quay in use: Bristol's Museums, Galleries and Archives.
p.27   Shadow of tower crane on Hannover Quay: Bristol's Museums, Galleries and Archives.
p.33   Painting of The Great Crane by William Halfpenny: Bristol's Museums, Galleries and Archives.

Design and artwork by Thomas Rasche
Printed by HSW Print, Tonypandy

Contents

Floating Harbour

Bristol is situated on two rivers: on the Frome and the Avon, with good access to the Severn Estuary. It was located where the two rivers met, near to Bristol Bridge. Then in 1247, as a considerable achievement, the Frome was redirected to its new course, known now as St Augustine's Reach. This runs between today's Bordeaux Quay and Narrow Quay and under Pero's bridge (the horned bridge). This enabled the city to be accessible by boat from two sides. Queen Square was a marsh, and the city's enclosing wall was just to the north of it.

By 1581, Bristol is shown in Georgius Hoefnagle's map to have boats on both sides of the city. 'The Kay' was the name of the (newish) dockside on the Frome, currently Broad Quay (at the head of St Augustine's Reach, with the fountains). The other quay was 'ye Backe', currently known as Welsh Back, beside Bristol Bridge with boat moorings. Queen Square was still a marsh and outside of the city, but a building is indicated where the current Stephen Joyce statue of John Cabot is located, next to the Arnolfini (Cabot had already discovered Newfoundland by 1497). This building indicates some activity here, a part of the Avon that had a steeper bank, located on the concave, and therefore deepest, part of the river. This location had been known as the Gibtaylor, as written by William Wycestre in 1480. Historical documents refer to Bristol's Gibtaylor during the visit by Elizabeth I in 1574, and as a drowning location for captured Arabs by Oliver Cromwell in the 1640s.

In 1673, James Millerd's map indicates a growing city. Queen Square had become a bowling green, and Redcliffe (the red cliffs give the name), located just across Bristol Bridge, was expanding. In 1750, John Rocque's map shows three distinct river fronts: The Key (Broad Quay), The Back (Welsh Back) and The Grove (named after the trees planted there). Furthermore, on The Grove, the first constructed dock has appeared at what is the **Mud Dock**, next to the location of the Great Crane. This location is exactly where the current iron jib crane is situated. Queen Square had also been constructed by this time.

Opposite: extract from John Millerd's Map 1673, with Alice Chester's (?-1485) crane, the first crane location on a map. The Bridge is now Bristol Bridge. Marsh gate is in the city wall, which runs behind the King Street buildings.

The industrial revolution created canals, rail and roads, making inland transport a viable alternative to coastal transport. Until then, boats were the cheap, quick, safe and reliable way to transport goods and travel in Britain.

In Benjamin Donn's map of 1773, a new East Mud Dock is shown, as well as docks on the opposite side of the Avon: there is an inlet or dock where the current Bathurst Basin passage is located (next to the Ostrich Inn). On one side of the inlet, the 1780 map by Barrett shows 'Trin Mill' next to the current Merchants Quay, and on the other side is Redcliffe Parade, on the cliff top. Elsewhere, located at **Prince's Wharf**, a few docks are constructed, including a dry dock. On these maps, Canon's Marsh appears, belonging to Augustine Canons Abbey Church (founded 1142 and to become Bristol Cathedral), located at **Hannover Quay**. By 1794, Mathews's map shows Canon's Marsh with Sea Banks enclosing the marsh and inlets off the Frome: the first indication of development.

With increasing activity, the harbour of Bristol was busy and under strain. A method to resolve this was at first proposed by William Milton in 1791, but then an engineered proposal was put forward by William Jessop in 1802. This was the proposal for what is now known as the Floating Harbour: a tide protected area around the centre of Bristol. This allows continuous loading and unloading, independent of the height of the tide, increasing the harbour's capacity and efficiency. The plan involved creating a new route for the river Avon, south of the city (The New Cut), and putting in dams or locks at Cumberland Basin, Bathurst Basin and Temple Meads. It was opened in May 1809. This was a radical improvement in the efficiency of the city's quays.

The harbour needed more improvements. In 1832, Brunel suggested improved methods of clearing the silt at the bottom of the harbour: four sluices to work in conjunction with a dredger. This was done together with the construction of the Underfall yard. In 1848, the Corporation took over from the Bristol Dock Company, so that the dues could be reduced for the commercial use of the harbour. Jessop's 1809 locks were only 13.7m (45ft) wide, so Brunel built a new lock at Cumberland Basin in 1849 which was 16.5m (54ft) wide. In the 1870s, as steam-engine coasters outgrew the capacity of many ports, they concentrated their traffic on bigger harbours including Bristol, adding more pressure. The locks were now too small, so in 1873 Thomas Howard built an 18.9m (62ft) wide lock.

Developments continued with increasing traffic and size of boats. In particular, it was an increase in the number of cargo vessels, whereas the size of passenger vessels began to outgrow Bristol's harbour. Cargo vessels remained operationally efficient (crew and loading times) at a smaller scale and tonnage, until the introduction of containers.

Howard's locks, built 1873 are still in use.

Brunel's lock enlargement, built 1849, with curved walls, visible at low tide.

Railway around to Canon's Marsh, built 1906.

River Avon

Cumberland Basin

Junction locks in Rownham Dam

Floating Harbour

Jessop's locks built 1809. To the Avon, the north lock is now filled in, but the entrance is still visible. The south lock was enlarged by Brunel. Only one junction lock was built.

Underfall Yard: hydraulics powered the docks, including cranes and swing bridges. It also has sluices to clear mud from the harbour. Built in the 1880s.

Ashton swing bridge, a double decker bridge: with cars on top and rail below, built 1906. Now a foot/cycle bridge.

New Cut, built 1809

An illustration of the problem of passenger vessels outgrowing Bristol's harbour was Brunel's SS *Great Britain*, the world's largest ship at its launch in 1843. It could only leave the harbour once the coping stones on the quay were removed. It was 14.6m (48ft) wide compared to the lock's 13.7m (45ft). The vessel heralded the new use of iron and propellers.

In the meantime, technology improvements were continually introduced to the harbour: more cranes, more quaysides and railway lines. With the 1803 Warehousing Act, boats could be offloaded directly into warehouses, though this was initially only used in London St Katherine's docks in 1828.

In Ashmead's map of 1855, Canon's Marsh is shown with the construction of Liverpool Wharf. At this location, the Hannover Quay crane tower appears on the 1886 OS map, together with a timber yard and railway lines.

The 1886 OS map demonstrates a considerable quayside development. Prince's Wharf is built over, together with railway lines and sheds. There is a rail connection directly from Wapping Wharf, past the back of Prince's Wharf sheds, to Temple Meads. This rail crossed the current Bathurst Basin passage where the footbridge is located. The railway lines can still be seen on the ground, next to the Ostrich Inn, as well as the tunnel entrance under Redcliffe Hill. The Fairbairn Steam Crane, constructed on **Wapping Wharf**, served the port's modernisation.

With the Avonmouth docks and the opening of the new Royal Portbury docks in 1977, Bristol's commercial harbour trade reduced and then ceased, in the mid-1970s.

Isambard Kingdom Brunel (1806-1859) is a key figure in the history of Bristol and the Floating Harbour. He played a part in the harbour construction, its redundancy and then also its rejuvenation. He constructed curved-wall locks in Cumberland Basin (they can still be seen at low tide). His ship SS *Great Britain* was a first suggestion that the city docks were becoming too small. This same ship became a symbol of the reinvention of the floating harbour as a tourist attraction, after it was salvaged from the Falkland Islands and returned to Bristol in 1970.

In 2000, the Frome was restyled again (excavated/redirected in 1247, part filled in 1892 for trams and in 1937 for roads) as part of the harbourside regeneration project. This includes dockside regeneration, developments and the opening of the Museum of Bristol (M-Shed) in 2011. The Floating Harbour celebrated its 200th anniversary in 2009.

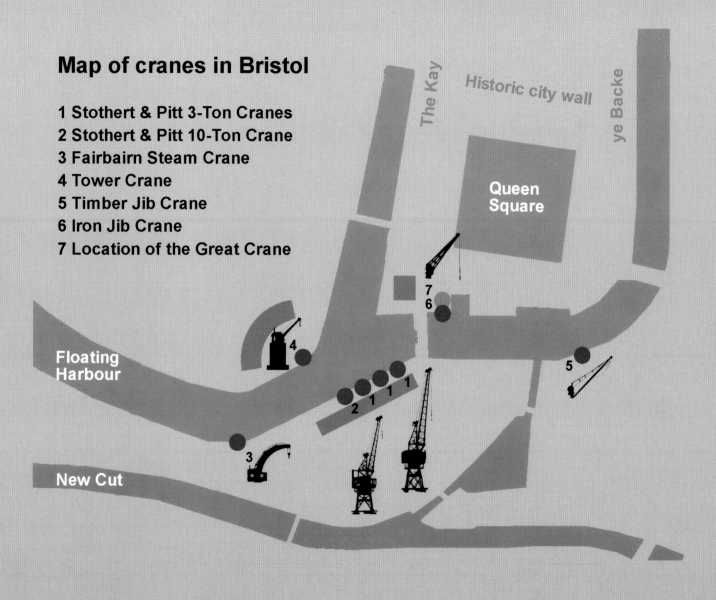

Map of cranes in Bristol

1 Stothert & Pitt 3-Ton Cranes
2 Stothert & Pitt 10-Ton Crane
3 Fairbairn Steam Crane
4 Tower Crane
5 Timber Jib Crane
6 Iron Jib Crane
7 Location of the Great Crane

The Kay

Historic city wall

ye Backe

Queen
Square

7
6

Floating
Harbour

4

2 1 1 1

5

3

New Cut

Crane types

The cranes covered in the chapters of this book are dockside cranes of Bristol harbour that are still standing, as well as the former Great Crane. Bristol once had many cranes of many different types. The dockside cranes were used to offload cargo from boats. Others included ship-mounted cranes/derricks, shipyard cranes for the construction of boats, gantry cranes and mobile cranes (on non-rail wheels).

Cab	the location of the crane operator.
Capstan	rotating machine (usually vertical) used to apply force to ropes and cables.
Crank handle	handle to manually power a crane (to hoist or slew).
Derrick	structural arm which is hinged freely at the bottom, supported by ropes (usually on board ships).
Gantry	bridged and supported at both ends. A gantry crane runs horizontally, used in cargo dockyards.
Gibbet	upright post with an arm (shape of a hangman).
Hoist	the vertical lifting of a load.
Jib	the structural reaching arm of the crane.
Luff	lifting or lowering the jib. If the hook remains at the same height as the jib lifts, it is level-luffing.
Pinion	the small gear in a gear train.
Pulley	or 'block and tackle' is the use of a wheel (sheave) to gain mechanical advantage, at the hook etc.
Quay	wharf built parallel to the shoreline.
Ratchet, pawl	a toothed wheel (ratchet) with a hinged catch (pawl), permitting movement in one direction only.
Slew	the jib (and cab) turn around, rotating the jib over the water and land.
Tower	a vertical construction, creating a higher platform from which a crane can operate.
Treadwheel	a wheel turned by walking within it. It has mechanical advantage over manual power.
Trestle	the arrangement of the main post and supporting structure for a Rat's Tail crane or Post Windmill.
Trundle	small wheel or roller.
Wharf	landing place or pier where ships may tie up and load or unload.
Windlass	horizontal cylinder (barrel) which is rotated by the turn of a crank or belt.

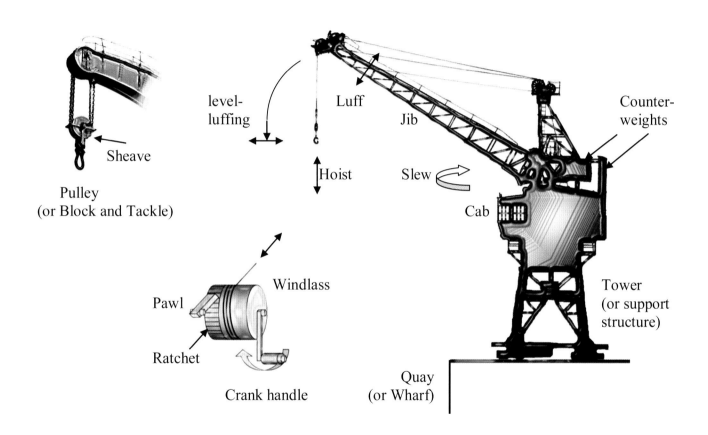

Pulley
(or Block and Tackle)

Sheave

level-
luffing

Luff

Jib

Counter-
weights

Hoist

Slew

Cab

Tower
(or support
structure)

Pawl

Windlass

Ratchet

Crank handle

Quay
(or Wharf)

When looking at cranes, it is useful to know what to look for. In particular, as they are functional objects, their construction always has a reason. Cranes reflect the circumstances in which they were used and the technology of their time. The crane is useful if it is strong and able to lift (hoist) a big load.

The strength of a crane depends on the strength of cable (rope or chain), the pulling power and its stability. The strength of the pulling power can be improved with a stronger engine, or with mechanical advantage, such as using treadmills rather than crank handles, a pinion wheel turning a larger wheel in a gear train and pulleys to reduce the load on a rope. The strength of the crane as a whole depends on the construction materials, for the jib, gears and other parts. However, an interesting aspect is how the crane is kept stable, especially if it moves or rotates.

Moving objects out of a boat and onto the quay usually requires a horizontal turning or slewing movement. As this is only one rotation, it is possible to fix the crane in the vertical axis. This can be seen with the use of the trestle posts, the fixing points of the Great Crane and the foundations of the timber jib crane, the iron jib crane and especially with the underground supporting structure of the Fairbairn crane.

A slewing crane can be made stable with a solid fixing, but this is not possible if the crane needs to travel or have other movements. Stability is then only possible with balance and counter-balance. The Stothert and Pitt cranes at Prince's Wharf demonstrate this solution very well. The greater the loads lifted, the greater the counter balances required. Furthermore, a crane's stability is particularly affected by its height and reach. These act like levers, pulling at the crane and making it unstable. A crane with a short height and reach (e.g. Fairbairn crane) is strong but stubby looking, unlike a tall, far reaching and economically designed one (e.g. Stothert and Pitt cranes).

Every crane tells a story.

Cranes can be designed to be strong or far reaching, anchored or balancing, fixed or moving. Their design reflects the contemporary understanding of technology and mechanics, with the use of materials such as wood or metal in the construction. Furthermore, each part is again a reflection of technology: a rope or chain, pulley or gears, rivets or welds. The energy required is provided by human, horse, steam, hydraulic and electric power, with these all requiring a number of dedicated operators.

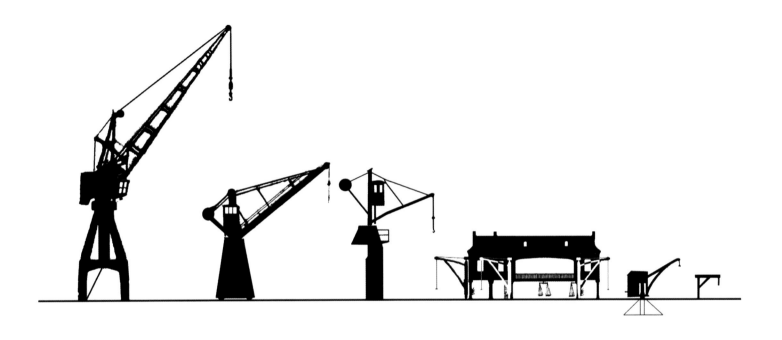

| S&P DD2, Wapping Wharf | Armstrong Hydraulic, Narrow Quay | Hydraulic, fixed to sheds Bordeaux Quay | Great Crane, Mud Dock | Rat's Tail, Narrow Quay | Gibbet, Narrow Quay |

7

The silhouettes of some of the cranes that used to be seen in Bristol docks: now demolished

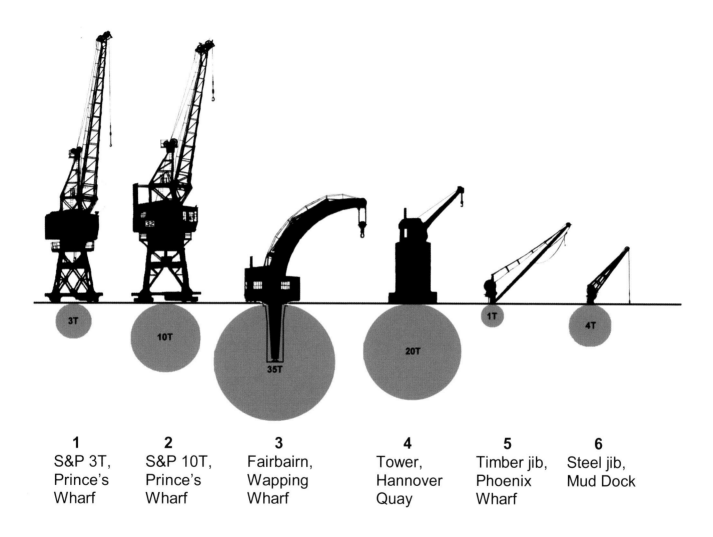

1	**2**	**3**	**4**	**5**	**6**
S&P 3T, Prince's Wharf	S&P 10T, Prince's Wharf	Fairbairn, Wapping Wharf	Tower, Hannover Quay	Timber jib, Phoenix Wharf	Steel jib, Mud Dock

The silhouettes of the cranes that can be seen in Bristol docks, with their lifting loads

Loading and unloading

All cranes are designed for the purpose of loading and unloading heavy goods. In a dock, the loading is from a boat to the quayside and vice versa. There are many different types of boats and many different ways to move the load once on the quayside. The ships visiting Bristol included merchant, passenger and some naval vessels. Most loading by cranes was done for merchant ships with bulky cargo, whereas passengers required less crane usage.

In a coastal country like Britain, boats were the most efficient way of carrying goods around. The best method was to pack the goods into smaller containers that could be transported by hand, in conjunction with bringing the boats as close to their destination as possible, thereby minimising transport distances. If the loads weren't loose, they were put into sacks that could be carried (e.g. coal and grain), or into barrels (for liquids) that could roll. Bristol had two quaysides in the city, with a short distance from boat to destination. St Nicholas Back (currently Welsh Back) had the first crane to be located on a map, located within Bristol's city walls (see James Millerd's 1673 map, p.5).

To offload a boat onto the quayside, a winding or gibbet crane would hoist the loads, which were then placed on horse-drawn (or dog) sleds, as Samuel Pepys described in his diary of 1668, and Philip van Dijk painted around 1760. A sled moves well on smooth granite cobbles, is low to the ground (less height to lift) and has no wheel vibration. The reach of a gibbet crane is neither far nor high (it works as a hoist), so a sled can quickly move a lot of material away from the quayside. Bristol's high tidal range (12m!) required quick unloading, with much hoisting.

The ships that first served Bristol were trows, flat-bottomed cargo vessels, suited for shallow water and being grounded at low tide. The generic term for a sailing boat used around the coast was a coaster, general cargo and passenger vessels. Coal was a major cargo, so colliers were used for the transport of loose coal. These colliers were unloaded by using lighters (barges without power, used to take cargo from a ship, thereby making it lighter, floating higher in the water), with a technique called coal-whipping: the coal was hoisted by basket and pulley, with men called 'whippers' hauling at the other end of a rope, using their weight as momentum to run the load up and down.

Opposite: *Bristol Docks and Quay* (courtesy of Bristol's Museums, Galleries and Archives), attributed to Philip van Dijk c.1760: Broad Quay with sleds, rat's tail and gibbet cranes.

Ships can be defined by purpose or type. Prior to the eighteenth century, merchant ships were classified by their hulls, with each type describing the location of the masts. In the eighteenth century, the hulls became more similar, so ships were defined more by their rigs: how the sails are arranged on a number of masts. The sails are either perpendicular to the keel (square) or aligned with it (fore-and-aft). The rigs of the ships in Bristol were various, but typical was a brig or brigantine, which was defined as a merchant-ship with two masts (William Falconer in 1780). Also typical were three (or more) masted barques and full-rig ships. In 1497, Cabot sailed a Portuguese caravel, a three-masted ship with a lateen rig. A lateen rig is a fore-and-aft rig, whereby a triangular sail hangs from a sloping 'yard' (beam), which hangs off a mast. Sailing ships were used until the mid-19th century.

Early cranes were effective if they could reach a few metres over the side of a boat, as the task was principally to hoist goods. A long-reaching crane is weaker and its slew may be obstructed by a ship's rigging. The innovations in cranes were mostly in lifting strength (mechanical advantage of levers and gears) as well as brakes. The major changes for the cranes occurred at the time of the industrial revolution. In particular, this brought with it new materials, power and shipbuilding technology. From 1809, Bristol had the new Floating Harbour to counter the high tidal range of the Avon. The emphasis changed from hoisting to loading time and from quays used for laying-up (idle ships tied side by side) to quays used for cargo handling. It was the time for efficiency: faster and continuous offloading, more power (steam) and volumes of cargo. By the late 19th century, more ship's deck cranes were in use than dockside cranes. Big iron ships had steam power with more cargo space and fewer crew.

Further developments for cargo included the 1803 Warehousing Act, which enabled ships to be unloaded directly into warehouses and the 1876 Plimsoll Shipping Act prevented boats being overloaded. By the 1840s, steam ships were in the ascendant, especially as passenger ferries.

The last innovation was to pack cargo into containers, so that any kind of object could be transported in bulk. Containers require huge cranes and big ports, but unfortunately, Bristol could not offer these. The Avon and the Floating Harbour had limits, e.g. 91m (300ft) length to get around the horseshoe bend in the Avon, and the lock sizes. Commercial traffic left Bristol, and with this the unloading of ships became redundant.

Opposite: Hannover Quay tower crane lifting a wing section of the Saunders-Roe *Princess* flying boat, March 1950.

Stothert & Pitt Cranes

The four Stothert & Pitt Cranes are located on Prince's Wharf.
Three are Stothert & Pitt 3-ton cranes, built in 1951; the other is a Stothert & Pitt 10-ton crane, built in 1950.

These four cranes are the showpiece cranes of Bristol Harbour. They are highly visible and they form part of the working exhibits of the Bristol City Museum.

The cranes can be operated by one person (they were known colloquially as Tin Gods) from the cab. This operator can control the travel (movement along the railway), slew (turning the crane), hoist (three-speed lifting and brake) and luffing (lifting the jib). Further workers are required at the hook end of the crane. These cranes were built using the strength and speed advantages of electric power (using three motors) and the development of railways. Furthermore, the cranes were level-luffing, with a loading capacity to their full reach. Level-luffing cranes use less energy, as no extra lifting of the load takes place during the luff. These were extremely effective cranes.

These cranes are witness to the increased vessel sizes and developments in speed and efficiency of unloading logistics. They also saw the end of Bristol harbour as a centre of commerce, with Prince's Wharf part of the last general cargo berth in the Bristol docks before commercial traffic moved to the Avonmouth and Royal Portbury Docks on the Severn estuary.

S&P 3-Ton cranes

¿ Lifting capacity
3 tons (limited by size)

¿ Toppling over
The jib reaches 20m, with
load capacity up to full reach.
Crank jib with counterweights.
Tall and on rails limits lift loads.

¿ Clearance
Lift height 20m
Tall enables good clearance,
over quay and onto boats.
Reach is 20m from axis.
4m to quay edge.
Level luffing.
360° slewing.
Slew onto railway and road.

¿ Materials
Riveted steel construction.
Latticed jib.
Steel lifting cable with hook.
415V Electric power.

Stothert & Pitt are crane manufacturers who originated as ironmongers in 1785. They had their workshop in Newark Street, Bath, but as they grew, they moved to Lower Bristol Road, Bath. Now, the company has an address in Brislington, Bristol and is a division of the Clarke Chapman Group. Stothert & Pitt built Britain's first electric dockside crane for Southampton in 1893.

There were variations and developments in the designs of cranes in the Bristol docks. Many of the smaller capacity general cargo cranes were replaced with newer cranes, as crane technology developed. They became more flexible, able to cope with heavier or more specialised cargo. For example, a specialised crane was at Pool's Wharf which was stockier, used to unload the sand dredgers, such as the *Harry Brown*. In the 1880s, a dockside water-hydraulic system was in use, with steam power for heavy loads. From the 1920s, electricity became the most important power source. The most advanced cranes in use were the S&P DD2 cranes built in 1959. These are tall and have a welded tubular steel construction, not a rivetted lattice. These were moved to Portishead in 1962 and are still in use.

The numbers 29-32 on the sides of the cranes indicate that Bristol docks had many cranes in use. In the 1950s, there were over forty in the city docks (an equal number to Avonmouth). The cargo cranes often worked very closely together on the quaysides.

The surviving cranes are currently undergoing restoration work and will feature as major working exhibits for the Museum of Bristol, due for completion in 2011.

S&P 10-Ton crane

¿ Lifting capacity
10 tons (extra stability with a large counterweight)

¿ Toppling over
The jib reaches 17m, with load capacity up to full reach. Crank jib with counterweights. Extra counterweight behind cab.

¿ Clearance
Lift height 20m
Tall enables good clearance, over quay and onto boats.
Suits large boat sizes.
Reach is 17m from axis.
4m to quay edge.
Level luffing.
360° slewing.
Slew onto railway and road.

¿ Materials
Riveted steel construction.
Latticed jib with stay cables.
Steel lifting cable with hook.
415V Electric power.

Fairbairn Steam Crane

The Fairbairn Steam Crane is located on Wapping Wharf. The design was originally patented by Sir William Fairbairn (1789-1874) in 1850.

This patent had run out, so it was free to be used. It was built for the docks by Stothert & Pitt in 1878. The construction also included the well-keyed stone foundation works extending out of Wapping Wharf.

Unfortunately, despite the care taken to build the foundations, the crane was too low for adequate clearance above the water. As boats became bigger, and with the construction of the Floating Harbour in 1809, there were no more height advantages obtained from the tide.

In 1892 hydraulic cranes arrived in Bristol, followed by the electric cranes in 1906. These new cranes were strong, faster and more flexible than the Fairbairn crane, which typically took $1\frac{1}{4}$ hours per lift. At most, the crane was used about twice a month, with the exception of a fully booked two-year period during WWII.

The crane is powered by two steam engines: hoist and slew (though slewing can also be done by hand). There are two brakes, a foot brake for the hoist. One operator can control the two engines, working with a banksman (at the hook). Despite being the oldest crane in 1950, its strength meant it was the only crane initially able to unload containers.

This crane is now assigned a Scheduled Ancient Monument status by the Department of the Environment.

¿ Lifting capacity
   35 tons
   Chains and pulley indicate strength.

¿ Toppling over
   The jib reaches 10.7m, with
   load capacity up to full reach.
   Foundation post 4.6m deep.
   No counterweight or stay cables.

¿ Clearance
   Lift height 12.2m
   Suits heavy, awkward loads.
   Reach is 10.7m from axis.
   2m to quay edge.
   360° slewing.
   Slew directly onto quay and railway.
   No luffing.

¿ Materials
   Riveted wrought-iron construction.
   Tubular jib, without stay cables.
   Lifting chains with pulley.
   Steam power.

Tower Crane

The Tower Crane is located on Hannover Quay, on the edge of Canon's Marsh. It was built as a steam crane in 1891 by A. Chaplin & Co. of Glasgow. Drawing on the experience with the Fairbairn crane, this crane was built on top of a tower to achieve greater height. Its construction coincided with the planned Great Western Railway connection across the Rownham Dam. Canon's Marsh was well suited for heavy cargo, as it was flat for rail and had a quayside suitable for steam-powered ships, with two long quaysides.

Only the tower now remains of this crane, located in the semi-circular space in front of the Lloyds TSB building. This is a prime location, intended as a focus for Bristol events and celebrations. Unfortunately, the tower looks awkward here, as the small weather vane on the top of it is out of proportion, the tower is not identifiable as a crane and it has not been reinvented with a new purpose.

The quayside along Canon's Marsh was constructed after the construction of the Floating Harbour of 1809. In Ashmead's map of 1855, quays and docks on Canon's Marsh sea banks had been partly constructed, with the location of this crane marked as Liverpool Wharf. In 1886, the OS map indicates timber yards and numerous cranes, and in the 1903 OS map, a marble works was located behind the crane. In 1922, a large warehouse was built behind the crane, 'No. 29 Bond', for Canon's Marsh Tobacco Bonds Ltd. The Tobacco Bonds building was demolished in 1988. With the harbourside regeneration, the quayside was lowered. The platform surrounding the base of the tower is the original height of the quay.

¿ Lifting capacity
20 tons
Tower provides a strong foundation.

¿ Toppling over
The tower serves as a solid foundation for the crane.
No counterweight, so the crane needs to have a solid base.

¿ Clearance
Extra height with tower.
Tower is 7.5m high.
Lift height c. 15m
Reach was 6m from axis.
2m to quay edge.
360° slewing.
Slew directly onto quay and railway.

¿ Materials
Steam power.
Stone tower.

Opposite: the tower on Hannover Quay with the crane 'ghosted in'.

Timber Jib Crane

The Timber Jib Crane is located on Phoenix Wharf. This crane was suited for self-operation, not needing an official operator. A crane is shown at this location on the 1903 OS map.

The mechanism is operated and powered with removable crank handles which operate the hoisting and slewing of the crane.

This quay was built, and appears on Ashmead's map of 1813-28, after the construction of the floating harbour of 1809. It was called Alfred Wharf, after King Alfred, who is said to have sheltered in the caves. In 1826, it was renamed King Wharf, after the owners, the King family. The 1886 OS map names this as Alfred Quay, and then the 1903 OS map shows this to be Midland Wharf, named after the railway company. A railway line used to run through the cliffs, under the church gardens and crossing the Bathurst basin where the current footbridge is located, beside Guinea Street. With recent renovation, it was renamed Phoenix Wharf (the former name of Sun Alliance Insurance Group).

Further round the Avon, Redcliffe Wharf is flat, making it a more useful and accessible quayside. A slip can be found, between this crane and the Bathurst basin that descends into the river. Between this slip and the slip opposite (under the riverstation restaurant) the Grove ferry used to cross.

The crane is in a state of disrepair and not functional.

¿ Lifting capacity
c.1 ton
Limited by rope strength and reach.

¿ Toppling over
The jib reaches 6m
Jib supported by jib stays.
Foundation in quayside.
No counterweight.

¿ Clearance
Lift height ca.15m.
Reach is 7m from axis.
2m to quay edge.
360° slewing.
Slew directly onto quayside.
No luffing.

¿ Materials
Steel mechanics.
Timber jib with stays.
Lifting rope.
Hand powered, with gears.

Iron Jib Crane

The Iron Jib Crane is located on Mud Dock, next to the site of the Great Crane and Prince Street bridge. In use, this was operated by one dock employee using crank handles.

This crane is number 12 of 21 locations shown on Ashmead's map of 1813-28, counting from Narrow Quay to the Backs ferry (the current location of Redcliffe bridge). The old wooden cranes at these locations were removed or replaced with iron cranes in the mid to late 19th Century. The 1886 OS map shows a crane here, next to 'Mud Dock West' (Ashmead's map called this the 'Old Mud Dock'). The 'Mud Dock East' ('New Mud Dock') had been built later. It was further developed c.1900 and the *Thekla* boat is now moored there.

The mechanism is operated and powered with removable crank handles, for the hoisting and slewing of the crane. Clearly visible is the brake handle with lock mechanism and the strong foundation in the quay. In part, the foundation fixing has a spread because the crane is so close to the quay edge. The crane uses gears for mechanical advantage, converting manual work into lifting strength.

There used to be a ferry crossing at the location of the Prince Street bridge. Two piers with gates were built here to divide the Floating Harbour in two. The hydraulic swing bridge, spanning the piers, had its foundation stone laid in 1808 and completed soon after the Floating Harbour. The bridge first appears on Ashmead's map of 1813-1828.

¿ Lifting capacity
4 tons
Small and stocky crane.

¿ Toppling over
The jib reaches 4m
Secure foundation in quayside.
No counterweight or stay cables.

¿ Clearance
Lift height ca.10m.
Reach is 5m from axis.
1m to quay edge.
360° slewing.
Slew directly onto quayside.
No luffing.

¿ Materials
Cast-iron crane.
Lifting chain.
Hand powered, with gears.

The Great Crane

The Great Crane was located on Mud Dock, one of the oldest quaysides in Bristol. Originally beyond the city walls, a building appears on Georgius Hoefnagle's map of 1581. This area came to be called 'ye Gibb' in James Millerd's map of 1673, and a rectangular dock appears in John Rocque's map of 1750.

The 'Great Crane' was built by John Padmore (c.1700-c.1740) in 1735. Until then, mostly gibbet and Rat's Tail cranes were seen in the docks. Padmore improved Rat's Tail cranes with the combination of a brake-drum, ratchet and pawl, as well as iron parts. However, he is remembered mostly for his construction of the Great Crane.

Cargo was usually in barrels and sacks. This crane offers three independent jibs for these, powered by treadmill or windlass within the crane housing. Innovations included the use of cast iron in mechanics and building (an important early use) and morticed cogs around the treadmills which mesh with a horizontal pinion. This enabled effective braking by the combination of a ratchet and pawl and a band brake. The rope wrapped around the axis of a treadwheel gives good mechanical leverage. The crane's operational end was the early 1800s, with the construction of the floating harbour.

Opposite: Painting by William Halfpenny in 1747, looking west. Mud Dock is visible on the left. The crane is loading a lighter. Behind the crane is the ferry slipway (now Prince Street/bridge), beyond is the Rat's Tail (or 'Rat Tailed') crane, in the direction of Arnolfini. Courtesy of Bristol's Museums, Galleries and Archives.

¿ Lifting capacity
Three jibs.
Strength not known.

¿ Toppling over
The jibs are hinged top and bottom, fixed securely to the building.

¿ Clearance
Lift height c.5m.
Reach is c.3m from axis.
Located on the quay edge.
180° slew of jib only.
Slew directly onto quayside.
No luffing.

¿ Materials
Timber.
Key parts with cast iron.
Lifting rope.
Treadmill powered.

THE Great Crane
at the Gate of Bristol
ERECTED
by Mr John Padmore
In the year 1735

Further reading

BIAS (Bristol Industrial Archaeological Society) journal volume 8, 1975 'Bristol Cranes'. Includes an article on John Padmore's cranes by Martin Watts and the Fairbairn crane by David Jones.

Stothert & Pitt: Cranemakers to the World, by Ken Andrews and Stuart Burroughs. Tempus Publishing and Arcadia Publishing. ISBN 9780752427942.

The Evolution of a Family Firm: Stothert and Pitt of Bath, by Hugh Torrens. Published by Stothert & Pitt, ISBN 0950602507. A book published by the crane makers themselves in 1978.

Animal-powered Machines, by J. Kenneth Major. Published by Shire Publications Ltd.: ISBN 0852637101, and *Britain's Working Coast in Victorian and Edwardian Times*, by John Hannavy. ISBN 0747806780. Two books of interest. Padmore's crane mechanism is described in *Animal-powered Machines*.

The Port of Bristol, by Andy King. The History Press Ltd. ISBN 0752427865. Stories and information about cranes, 'Tin Gods', as well as other images of various floating and dock cranes from the Bristol docks.

Discovering Harbourside: a journey into the heart of the city, by James Russell. Redcliffe Press Ltd. ISBN 9781906592315.

Bristol's Floating Harbour: The First 200 Years, by Peter Malpass and Andy King. Redcliffe Press Ltd. ISBN 9781906593285. The story of the Floating Harbour 1809-2009.

Bristol Then And Now, volume 2, by Janet and Derek Fisher. Bygone Bristol. ISBN 089938829X. Includes images of cranes on St Augustine's Reach and the shed at the location of the Great Crane.

From Bristol to the Sea: Artists, the Avon Gorge and Bristol Harbour, by Francis Greenacre. Redcliffe Press. ISBN 1904537391. With illustrations of The Great Crane, as well as Tower Crane, Rat's Tail and Gibbet cranes.

The Story of Bristol: From the Middle Ages to Today, by Bryan Little and John Sansom. Halsgrove Publishing. ISBN 1841143014.

Transport in Britain, 1750-2000: From Canal Lock to Gridlock, by Philip S. Bagwell and Peter Lyth. Hambledon Continuum. ISBN 1852855908. Describes transport for Bristol in a wider context.

Bristol: A People's History, by Peter Aughton. Carnegie Publishing Ltd. ISBN 1859360971.

Columbus Myth: Did Men of Bristol Reach America Before Columbus? by Ian Wilson. Simon & Schuster. ISBN 0671711679. Was America named after Richard Ameryk, the collector of customs for John Cabot...?

William Worcestre: The topography of Medieval Bristol [1480], by Bristol Records Society, Publication vol. 51. #253 he writes: "The crane [Alice Chester's], a public machine...well founded and firmly fixed into the ground".

Further information

Museum of Bristol (M-Shed), Princes Wharf, Bristol, Avon, BS1 4RN. Leaflets, information and exhibits. [From spring 2011]

Bristol's Museums, Galleries and Archives: Bristol Record Office, 'B' Bond Warehouse, Smeaton Road, Bristol. Historic maps, drawings and documents.

www.BristolCranes.co.uk

For further information about this book, ebook editions, cranes and more, visit the above website.

John Cabot thinking about Bristol's cranes...

www.redcliffepress.co.uk

For further information on Redcliffe Press Ltd., the publishers of this book, visit the above website.

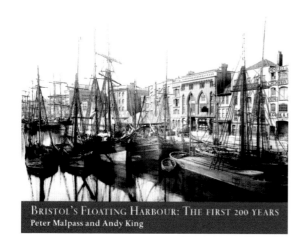

Forthcoming Bristol titles in 2010 include:

Discovering Bristol's Harbourside

Bristol's Best 100 Buildings

Also available as an e-book

www.BristolCranes.co.uk

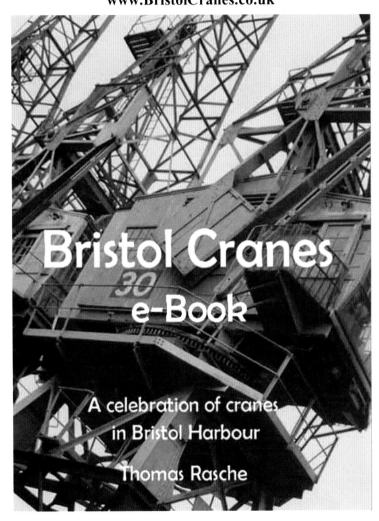

Bristol Cranes

e-Book

A celebration of cranes in Bristol Harbour

Thomas Rasche